WRITING PROMPTS DECODED:

CREATIVE PROMPT IDEAS TO CREATE CONTENT FOR YOUR FICTION BOOK

APRIL L. TAYLOR

REGAL PRESS

Writing Prompts Decoded: Creative Prompt Ideas

To Create Content For Your Fiction Book

Copyright © 2018 by APRIL L. TAYLOR

All rights reserved. No part of this publication may be reproduced, stored in a retrieval system, or transmitted by any means – electronic, mechanical, photographic (photocopying), recording, or otherwise – without prior permission in writing from the author.

To find out more about this book or the author, visit: www.authorapril.com

INTRODUCTION

So you want creative prompt ideas that you can use while writing your story? Do you want to create actual content for your fiction book? You are in the right place for that, my friend!

This is the fun introduction where I'll tell you what you need to know about writing prompts, why you should use them, and how to use the prompts in this book, but most importantly, I will tell you why this book is different from other writing prompt books. This isn't your typical book of writing prompts, but we will get to that later.

First, what is a writing prompt? In its purest form, a prompt is a short passage of text or an image that provides a potential topic idea or starting point. Some prompts include instructions that explain the purpose and how to use it. Most prompts are geared toward creating new story ideas.

The prompts in this book go beyond generating initial ideas for a new book or story. They are designed to be used while writing your fiction book or story. But before we get into that, let's talk about some of the awesome reasons to use writing prompts.

Creativity

They are an efficient way to get your creative juices flowing and generate ideas that go beyond your first thoughts. Prompts are a starting point for moving past your initial ideas to get to the unique ones that will stand out and keep your readers turning the pages in anticipation.

Improve Skills & Techniques

Writing prompts allow you experiment with and improve writing techniques and skills. Each time you use a prompt, you are becoming a more experienced writer.

Lower Stakes = Higher Output

A prompt isn't as stressful as writing a great scene or story because the stakes are lower. This can remove the pressure and allow you to let go of perfection.

Confidence

If you commit to using writing prompts regularly, you will see a boost in your writing skill and confidence.

Power To Beat The Blank Page

Not sure what to write? Know what you should be writing but can't seem to get started? A prompt is a perfect way to set your writing muscles in motion. I like to think of prompts as the warm-up before the workout.

Find Your Style & Strengths

Using prompts aids you in developing your writing style and strengths. Experimenting with a variety of prompts will help you discover who you are as a writer and what your writing passion is.

WHY THIS BOOK?

That, my friend, is an excellent question. The idea for this book was born while I was working on the third draft of my fantasy novel. I love writing prompts, but I didn't want to spend my precious writing time on words that wouldn't end up in my book or at least make it better in some way.

Naturally, I started searching for writing prompts that I could use while writing my book. When I didn't find what I was looking for, I started creating my own and sharing them with other writers.

With this book, you will create in-depth characters, stellar settings, killer conflicts, and master lists you can use for your next book. It contains creative prompt ideas that you will use to create actual content for your fiction book, including dialogue and action scenes.

You will love the creativity of using these creative prompts to improve your writing skills, without out feeling like you should be writing your book instead. That is because all of the prompts will either create book content, support your story, spur creativity, build your writing skills, or focus on problems you are having with your writing.

HOW TO USE THIS BOOK

The prompts are divided into categories to make them easy to use with your work in progress. You can jump to any section at any time or work through them from the beginning.

Some prompts will include detailed instructions while others are self-explanatory. Some will include examples, starter words, or information about the skill you are building when using such prompts. List building and mind mapping are suggested in some of these prompts. They are great tools for organizing ideas and spurring creativity. I have included links and resources about mind mapping in the *Writers Tool Kit* section in the back of the book.

While you will create actual content for your book with some of these prompts, others will create behind-the-scenes content. The actual writing from these prompts may not make it into your book, but it will strengthen your story or your writing in some way.

If a prompt instructs you to create a journal entry from your main character's point of view about their favorite childhood memory, you probably won't be including the journal entry in your novel. However, you can use emotions your character experienced, a flashback, or the lasting impact that it had on them.

Using these prompts in conjunction with your current writing will help you write a better book or story. This might come in the form of a new idea that transforms your plot. It could be a revelation about your character's motives based on their newly uncovered backstory or a change in setting that perfects the atmosphere of the story.

There are two chapters in this book geared toward helping you solve two common problems writers face. One is losing passion for your story, and the other is getting stuck or blocked while writing.

Check out the Writers Tool Kit section in the back of the book . You will find resources, links to apps and access to Writers Tool Kit videos.

Don't forget to sign up for my free monthly newsletter and get your bonus prompts.

One last thought before you get started:

I encourage you to keep all of the writings generated from these prompts even if they will never make it into your book or story. No words written are ever wasted because they make you a better writer. It is also smart to find other ways to use the content you create.

After all, you have already put in the effort! Can you turn it into a novella, a blog post, or bonus content for your email subscribers? If there is one thing I hope you take away from this book, it is that no writing, no matter how big or small, is ever a wasted effort.

Words matter. You matter. And your words matter!

Go forth, get creative and write content for your fiction book!

CHAPTER 1

PROMPTS FOR CREATING & DEVELOPING CHARACTERS

READERS WANT REALISTIC, believably flawed characters that they can relate to. Knowing your characters inside out allows you to present them accurately to the reader. These character prompts guide you to get up close and personal with your characters. You will flesh out the details of who they are, what they do, and why they do it.

1. Dear Diary

Create a journal or diary for your main character. Using their voice, write a week's worth of entries. This is a valuable tool for getting in touch with what is going on in their life before the inciting incident occurs.

2. Confessions

Write a letter from your character to a loved one, confessing a lie or a deep dark secret. Write a short scene that shows the character contemplating if they should mail the letter. Let the characters inner turmoil shine in your writing. Write a scene that involves the character discovering the letter was accidentally sent. Focus on showing the characters distress or relief. Is there a place in your own work in progress where you can weave in emotions of distress or relief? Will your character be making a confession of some kind in your book? If so, write or rewrite that scene to show the inner turmoil to the reader.

3. Get Sketchy

Draw a sketch of your character or search online for photos. Write a detailed description of their appearance.

4. Time to Pin

Create a Pinterest board for your main character. Pin images that they would pin. Pin clothing they would wear, the food they eat, and photos of their home and environment. You can include the character's inspiration images or the sketch. You can set your board to private so that you are the only one that can view it or keep it public to connect with readers.

5. Personality Tests

Personality tests are a great tool for developing characters. Find a free test online and answer the questions from your character's perspective. You can refer back to their personality type while writing. The choices they make in the story should be consistent with their personality type. For your convenience, I have included links to two of my favorite free personality test in the *Writers Tool Kit* section.

6. Lost and Late

Your character is lost in a place that is out of their typical element. They are late for a crucial event. It can't be rescheduled. Write a scene that shows how your character deals with this. Now, that you know how your character will react in a difficult situation you can look for ways to apply that reaction in your book. Check the scenes or chapters that you have already written and be certain your character is reacting consistently.

7. Fear Factor

Make a list of 10 things that scare your character. Select 3 and write a paragraph about each one, explaining the fear. This is an excellent time to develop a backstory for your character. Consider using those fears as possible conflicts in your story.

8. Dear Diary

Pull out your character's journal. Write an entry about a time that they were stood up by a date, let down by a parent, or disappointed by a friend. Dig deep into their emotions and write a scene that conveys those emotions.

9. Loyalty

Is your character loyal? Do they consider themselves loyal? If so, write about what would cause the character to be disloyal. Would they remain loyal if their spouse cheated? Would they betray a friend to save the life of a family member? Would they sacrifice loyalty for a large sum of money? Will their loyalty or lack of it play a part in your work in progress?

10. Jailbirds

Your character is in jail. What did they do to get there? Who will they call to bail them out? Who is in jail with them? What consequences will they face tomorrow, and how will they deal with that? This is another prompt that helps you go deeper into your characters motives, actions, and reactions.

11. Vacation Time

Your character is going on vacation. Where are they going? How will they get there? Who are they taking with them? Write a scene or journal entry that describes their experience.

12. Pretty Little Lies

Does your character consider themselves truthful? When do they think lying is okay? Jump into your character's mindset. Write a scene where the character is caught in a lie. How do they handle it? Do they come clean, make a joke, make up more lies, defend themselves, or throw the blame on someone else. Write 500 words explaining what your character lies about and why. How will your characters lies impact your plot?

13. Biggest Lie

Write about the worst, biggest lie that the character has ever told. Did they get caught? If not, who do they keep the lie from being discovered. Will this lie impact your plot? Will it impact how your character makes choices in your story? Has this part of their backstory shaped them into who they are when the story starts?

14. Lie Detector

Your character is taking a lie detector test. What questions do they hope won't come up?

15. Inner Lies

What lies does your character believe about themselves? How do these untruths impact them? How will these inner lies impact your plot? Will your character discover the truth by the end of your book?

16. Eye of The Beholder

Describe the character from another character's point of view. Contrast this to how the main character sees themselves.

17. Accusations

Your character is accused of something they did not do. Write a dialogue scene between them and the accuser. Include sensory details that show how the character is feeling.

19. Later

Make a list of things your character procrastinates about. Then expand on each one by making a list of the consequences of procrastinating. Will the characters procrastination tendency play a part in your work in progress?

19. Character Flaw Master List

Make a list of character flaws, starting with the letter A, and continue your list until you get to Z. This will give you a bank of flaws for your current and future characters.

20. Skills Master List

Create a master list of skills, talents, and abilities. Start with the things that are present in your current characters and continue to add to your list as you develop your characters.

21. Think Ahead

What skills does your character have now? How did the character obtain them? What skills does your character lack that will be needed later in the story? How and when will the character learn these skills?

22. Doorbells

The doorbell rings, but your character is not the mood to deal with guests. Who is at the door? What does your main character do? Ignore the bell? Creep around the house? Make someone else answer? Answer the door? This is a fun prompt that can give you more insight into how your character reacts. Do this prompt from the perspective of other characters in your story to make sure all of your characters are not having the same reactions.

23. Traitor

Your character suspects someone close to them is a traitor. How do they react? Write a scene

24. Risky Business

Your character has the chance to move up in their career, but it will mean risking their life and hurting someone they love. What do they do?

25. Zombie

It is an ordinary day. Your character is walking home and comes face-to-face with a zombie. How do they react? Fear? Disbelief? Humor?

26. Introvert or Extrovert?

Knowing if your character is a natural introvert or extrovert is important when you are writing. It will help you keep your character in character. If your character is an introvert, they will react differently to a crowd than an extrovert. Select an introvert and an exrovert from your story. Write a short scene from each characters point of view where they are dealing with the same situation.

27. Beauty In The Eye Of The Beholder

What one person sees as beautiful, another person may see as unattractive. For this prompt, make a list of 10 things your character finds beautiful. Pick one and write about it from your character's viewpoint. Then write about the same thing from the perspective of someone who finds it unattractive.

28. Treasure

What does your character treasure? Make a list of 10 things. Write about why those things are a treasure to them. What would cause the character to change their view about those things?

29. Trash

What is in your character's trash can? Spend a few moments writing about the items and how these things give insight into your character and their lifestyle. If your character is an alcoholic, his trash will look a little different from the trash of a single mom with 7 kids or teenager on the run from the police.

30. Career Master List

Create a master list of careers and jobs. Start by including all of the careers and jobs in your current book. Then continue brainstorming career possibilities. Next, examine how your characters career, job, or lack of one will impact your story. Pinpoint possible conflicts that arise or could arise in your story because of the characters career.

31. Write Your Inciting Incident Scene

The inciting incident is the force that makes your story happen. If this incident didn't occur your character wouldn't be forced to act and change. Write the inciting incident scene for you story. Then use these prompts to guide you.

- Does the inciting accident happen by choice or by accident? How does this impact your main character.
- Does your inciting incident fit with the genre you are writing?
- Does the incident allow your character to drive the plot?
- How will the character drive the plot forward because of the change?
- What promises and expectations are you presenting to the reader with this change?
- How will you meet the promise or expectation with the ending of your story?

CHAPTER 2

PROMPTS FOR CREATING CONFLICT

WITHOUT CONFLICT, you risk losing the reader. Every page of your story should have a conflict on some level. Use these prompts to explore conflict, practice building deeper levels of conflict and create content for your book:

1. Hero or Not?

Your character has a chance to rescue someone. The rescue will mean putting their life and goals in jeopardy. Write about the character's inner struggle of helping someone versus reaching their goal.

2. Conflict Assessment

Do a quick assessment of the conflict in your work in progress.

- Do you have both internal and external conflicts?
- Are there any spots in your story that lack conflict?
- Are there any conflicts that don't belong in your story?
- Do your subplots create conflict or intersect with the main conflict in the story?

3. Conflict Master List

Create your conflict master list. Start with problems or conflicts in your current story. Then set a timer. Spend 10–15 minutes adding more conflicts to your list. Don't judge your thoughts, edit, or backspace. Continue adding to your master list each time you think of a new conflict.

4. Fight

Write a scene involving your character and a longtime friend. They are fighting over something vital. This issue is putting their longtime friendship in jeopardy. End with a twist.

5. Violations

You character violated a company policy. Their intention was good, but they broke the rules. Write a dialogue scene between your character and the employer.

6. Taken

Pick something that is important to one of your characters and take it away from them. Write about what they have lost, how they are feeling, and what they intend to do about it. Apply what you learn about about your character and conflict to your story.

7. Worst Enemy

Is your character their own worst enemy? Make a list of all the possible ways the character can make this goal harder to achieve. Then write a scene that shows this to the reader.

Examples:

A. Your character wants to be accepted for who she is.

- But she never lets people get close enough to know her.
- But she acts tough and pushes people away.

- But she has amnesia and doesn't remember who she is.

B. Your character is searching for a lost friend.

- But he does it by breaking the law.
- But he is sabotaging his efforts by interrogating everyone who knew the friend.
- But he is kidnapped when he gets to close.

C. Apply it to your book.

- Select a conflict from your work in progress.
- List all the ways your character could make the conflict worse.
- Write or rewrite a conflict scene for your story.

8. Ransomed

Your character receives a strange ransom note. What does the note say, and what will your character do? Create a list of things that could make the conflict more difficult.

9. Up in flames

Everything in your character's life is going up in flames. A wizard gives your character a chance to save one thing from the fire, but there will be consequences. Who or what do they save? Why? What are the consequences, and do they regret it?

10. Switched

Your character finds two wrapped gifts on the porch of their cozy home. The instructions tell them not to open the gift until they give one away to a stranger. They give one to a homeless man. When opened, they each discover a plain red apple. Your character tosses their apple in the trash in disgust. The homeless man devours his with joy. The next day, your character finds that their life has been switched with the homeless man's. Write about what happens next. How does the new situation cause conflict for the character? How do they overcome it? What do they learn from it?

11. Opposites

Make a list of places that are opposites. Ocean vs. Desert, Dungeon vs. Tower. Select a character and place them in one location. Think about what their life would be like in that location. What would change about their life and goals if it took place in the opposite location? What would stay the same? What conflicts are dependent on the location? Then pick a scene or chapter in your story. Is the setting you have chosen the best setting? If not, change the setting, and rewrite it to make your story stronger.

12. Memory Share

Pick three childhood memories from your past. One positive, one negative, and one confusing. Pretend your character has similar memories. How would each of these memories affect them? What conflicts could arise from each of the memories?

13. The Winning Ticket

A positive event changes your character's life but not in the way they expected. What happens? It could be a birth, a gift, a wedding, a trip, or even a winning ticket. What outcome do they expect from the event? What happens instead? Contrast the expectation to the reality. This prompt helps you explore how your character's expectations can create a conflict.

14. Twisted

Your character went out of their way to do something good for someone, but things go wrong. The person they helped is twisting the story to make it seem your character was out to get them. Write about what happened and how your character will attempt to fix the situation.

What if his attempt to fix it makes it seem like the other person was right? How far can you escalate the problem for the character?

15. What If...

For the remaining prompts in the section use the *What If* method to take the conflicts to a deeper level. Keep asking and answering *What If* as long as you can. This will help you build the habit of seeking stronger conflicts when you write your current book or plot your next one.

Example Of *What If* Method:

Prompt: The package is lost in the mail.

- The package is lost in the mail.
- What if the package contains a murder weapon?
- What if the murder weapon was mailed as a threat?
- What if the wrong person receives the murder weapon?
- What if the person who received the weapon takes it to the police and the police arrest them for the murder?
- What if the real murder works at the police station?

16. What If

The barn is on fire.

17. What If

The castle appears haunted.

18. What If

A cursed treasure is unearthed in the backyard.

19. What If

The five leaf clover is bad luck.

20. What If

The monster looks like a normal person.

21. What If

Something deadly is crawling on your character.

22. What If

Your character is hiding from someone.

23. What If

Your character discovers their partner is cheating.

24. What If

Your character steals something.

25. What If

Your character causes an accident.

26. What If

Your character falls in the quicksand.

27. What If

The only way out is through the sewer.

28. What If

Your character witnesses a robbery.

29. What If

You character causes something to break.

30. What IF

Your character let the cat out of the bag.

31. Apply To Your Book

Use the *What If* method to check the conflicts and plot points in your story. Make a list of the existing conflicts and use the method to look for areas where you can deepen or strengthen your conflicts. Then rewrite or write a new conflict scene for your book.

CHAPTER 3
PROMPTS FOR SETTINGS

IT'S time to explore settings. Use these prompts to practice using settings to create atmosphere, mood, and conflict. Your setting should be more than just a place your characters exist.

1. Create a Master List Of Settings

Begin building a bank of settings. Set a timer for 15 minutes. List all the settings in your current project. Then move on to listing every possible environment, location, and place you can think of. Write each one down, no matter how silly, impossible, or irrelevant it seems. You won't use all these settings in your current story, but you are building an invaluable resource for your future stories. Trust me, you will thank me later.

2. Mind mapping

Select 3 settings from your setting master list. It's time for a bit of mind mapping. Write the setting in the center of a blank page. Circle it. Then write down everything that comes to mind about the setting.

Do this for each of the settings. You can also download a free mind mapping app from your app store if you prefer to work digitally.

3. Moods, Tone, & Atmosphere

Use a mind map to go deeper and get more specific. Expand on the details and ideas as much as possible. Create a setting that does more than give your characters a place to sit and stand. Consider the tone, themes, and moods you want to convey in your novel. How can you use each setting to show these things?

4. Get Conflicted

This prompt is all about finding ways to use a setting to move your story forward. Use it to create problems for the character that makes it difficult for them to get what they want. Use a mind map to brainstorm all the potential pitfalls, conflicts, and dangers that could arise from the settings.

5. Tour Guide

It is time to take your character on a tour of their surroundings. Begin by describing the sensory details. Focus on what the character sees, feels, tastes, smells, and touches as they tour the setting. Then read your description and circle all the words that stand out to you as bland or boring.

6. Expand & Improve

Write down the words you circled from number 5. Expand on these words. Find other synonyms and stronger descriptive terms to replace them. Use them to improve your description. When you move into the revision phase of writing your story; you can use this method to improve your writing.

7. Switch up

Pick a setting from your novel or experiment with a random setting from your master list. Write from the point of view of a first time visitor. The visitor is seeing the setting during the day and finds it comfortable and safe.

Next, rewrite the description to make the location seem scary, dangerous and uncomfortable. Do this by changing the adjectives.

This prompt makes you aware of how you can use the same setting in your story to create a different moods in different parts of your book.

8. X Marks the spot

Draw a map of your main settings. Don't focus on your drawing skills. Keep it simple. You need to know the layout of your settings to avoid confusing the reader.

9. Setting Mash Up

Use your list to mix and match settings to create more settings.

Here's a Sample Setting List:

- Flooring Showroom
- Coffee shop
- Abandoned Waterpark
- Foster Home
- Boarding school
- Farm
- Statue of Liberty
- Concert
- Open Mic Night
- Pizza party
- Dressing room
- Lemonade stand

Mash-Up Examples #1

Abandoned Water Park + Pizza Party

Play the *what if* game to come up with as many ideas as you can that mix 2 settings.

Abandoned Waterpark + Pizza Party

- *What if* some kids were having a pizza party in an Abandoned Waterpark?
- *What if* your character was exploring an abandoned waterpark?
- *What if* they came across a bunch of kids having a pizza party in the waterpark?

Mash-Up Example #2

Dressing Room + Concert

- *What if* your character sneaks into the dressing room of a performer while at a concert?
- *What if* your character started a new job cleaning up after a concert, and when he goes to clean the dressing room, there is blood everywhere?

Apply It To Your Story

- Can you create a stronger setting by adding another element of setting to it?
- Use the *What if* method to make sure you are using the best setting possible.

10. Strange Places & Objects

Your character is standing in the cemetery, holding a broken Christmas ornament. Write about the connection between the character, ornament, and cemetery. You can alter this prompt by changing the place and object.

11. Bird's-Eye View

Write about the same setting from the perspective of two very different characters. Focus on using the setting to show the characters emotions, perspective, and mood.

Example Prompts:

1. Setting: A fancy expensive restaurant

   - A. From the POV of an underpaid waiter who is behind on his rent and depressed because his girlfriend left him.
   - B. From the POV of a wealthy young woman who received a marriage proposal from her boyfriend.

12. Stormy Night Prompts

Use these three prompts to explore setting.

- It is the middle of the night. There is an epic storm brewing. You are somewhere you should not be. Write about where you are, what you are doing, and how you got there.
- It is the middle of the night. There is an epic storm brewing. Your characters are somewhere they should not be. Write about where they are, what they are doing, and how they got there.
- It is the middle of the night. There is an epic storm brewing. Your villain is somewhere they should not be. Write about where they are, what they are doing, and how they got there.

13. Camp Out

Write 3 scenes that takes place around a campfire. Include sensory details to show the mood and tone of each of the following scenes.

- A scared runaway teen living in the woods.

- Two old cowboys reminiscing about the good old days.
- A just married couple on their honeymoon.

14. I Spy

Your character is going to investigate something. Mix and match the suggestions below or create your own based on your story. Write a scene where the investigation goes wrong or a discovery is made.

What:

- *A crying child.*
- *A fallen tree.*
- *A strange noise.*

Where:

- *A park. A camper.*
- *A train.*
- *In an ice storm.*

When

- *After drinking too much at a party.*
- *On lunch break.*
- *During a funeral.*

15. Fear Street

What is your character afraid of? Make a list of places that they might come into contact with that fear.

Write about your character in that location coming face-to-face with their worst fears. Use the setting and sensory details to create a fearful atmosphere and mood.

16. Love Bug

Your character is in love. Who or what is the object of his/her affection? What does he/she want right now? What setting can make this problematic?

17. Not In Kansas Anymore

Your character wakes up in an unfamiliar place. Write a scene describing the character's confusion.

18. Time Traveler

Grab your character and stick them in a time machine. When and where do they end up? How does this new era and location change your character's goal and lifestyle?

19. Where In The World

Your character is inside something. The air around is moist. A bead of sweat rolls down their forehead. They press their hand against the gritty texture and force themselves to step forward. Where are they?

20. Night Vision

Your character steps outside at night. Write about what they see, hear, smell, and feel. Focus on using the sensory details to show the mood and tone of the scene.

What if the character stepped outside the next night, after a major change in their life—how would the change affect what they see, hear, smell, and feel?

Find a scene in your work in progress can you use sensory details related to the setting to invoke the mood and tone you want the reader to experience. Write the scene or revise it using sensory setting details.

21. Apply It To Your Story

You have explored settings, created your master list, and practiced weaving sensory details into your writing. Now, you are ready to get to work on your book. Use the following prompts as a guide:

- Pick a scene or chapter to write.
- Identify your settings.
- Identify the mood or tone that you want the reader to experience.
- Create a list of sensory details that are related to the setting. Make note of how you can use those details to set the tone and mood.
- Write or rewrite the scene or chapter using the setting and sensory details to show mood and tone.
- Are you using the setting to create conflict?
- Does the setting help to move your plot forward?
- Can the reader fully grasp where the character is?

CHAPTER 4
PROMPTS FOR WRITING ACTION SCENES AND PLOT TWISTS

IT IS time to focus on writing different types of scenes. In the following prompts you will use prompts to practice writing action scenes and plot twists. You will apply what you learn to your work in progress.

WRITE ACTION-PACKED SCENES

These prompts are action-focused. The goal is to practice writing action-filled scenes that will keep your reader on the edge of their seat. Try to avoid narration. Keep your pacing short.

1. Be The Hero

Search for real-life heroes online. Pick a hero or a fictional superhero to use for the following prompts and exercises.

Spend a few moments answering the following questions to get into the mindset of the hero:

- How did they save the day?
- Why did they do it?
- Did they prepare in advance or act in the moment?
- What did they think during the action?
- What were they feeling during the action?
- What did they think and feel afterward?
- Do they have any regrets?
- Think about the event taking place as the hero saves the day. What would the hero be experiencing at that moment? What would the hero feel, see, smell, and touch?

Set a timer for 10–15 minutes. Write about the event where the hero saves the day. Start at the exact moment the hero takes action. Focus on showing the reader what is happening. Keep the pace fast. Don't allow your hero to take a trip down memory lane to reflect on something from the past. Avoid writing things that stop the action. Keep the reader in the current moment.

2. Be The Damsel Or Dude In Distress

For this example, you are switching viewpoints from the hero to the person he/she rescued. You can use the same story from above or find a new one.

- What was the rescued person doing before they needed saving?
- What happened that caused them to need rescue?
- Who or what was responsible?
- Did the person in need play a part in their trouble?
- What were they thinking at the moment that the danger was clear to them?
- What emotions, body sensations, and sensory details did they experience before the rescue? During? Afterward?

Set the timer for 10–15 minutes. Write the action scene from the victim's point of view. Start at the moment they realize the danger. End at the moment they are safe. Keep your pacing tight by using short sentences. Include sensory details to draw the reader into the action.

3. Be the Villain or Criminal

If applicable, you can use the same story idea from above. A quick online search of recent news can provide a plethora of criminals to choose from.

- What crime did they commit?
- Why did they commit it?
- Was is pre-planned or at the moment?
- What was the criminal thinking and feeling right before committing the crime? During? Afterward?
- What sensory details will your villain experience during the crime?

Set your timer again. Start at the moment the criminal takes action to commit the crime. End when the villain is successful or when caught. Use sensory details and quick pacing to keep the action flowing.

4. Apply to Your Work in Progress

Now that you have practiced writing action-filled scenes, it is time to put it to work in your story. Pick an action scene in your book. You can write a new action scene or rewrite a scene to improve it.

Ask yourself these questions:

- What is the action?
- Who is making the action happen and why?
- Is your character in the role of hero, victim, or villain? If none of those apply, what is their role in the action happening?

- List all the actions that occurred in the scene. Then list the sensory details experienced during each action.

Set the timer. Write the scene. Focus on showing the action with short sentences. Use sensory details to show what the character is experiencing.

WRITING PLOT TWISTS

Your readers and your characters have expectations. Your job as a writer is to surprise them with something else. Don't you love it when you are reading a book and an unexpected plot twist makes you gasp out loud? That is the gift you want to give the reader. Having an outline of what is going to happen in your story will help you plan compelling plot twists if they do not naturally occur as you write. Use these prompts to practice building plot twists. Apply what you learn to your story.

5. Brainstorm

Pick a prompt. Set the timer for 10 minutes. Make a list of the ideas that come to mind. Your first thoughts will likely be that same thing the reader will expect. Your goal is to keep adding to the list until you have exhausted the obvious stuff. Set aside your first options. Set the timer for 10 minutes and keep brainstorming.

Select One:

- The building is on fire. The firefighters have not arrived.

Someone yells for help from the top floor. A pedestrian hears them and stops. What could happen next?
- A sudden storm catches the crew of the ship by surprise. What could happen next?
- The kidnapper grabs the child by the arm. What could happen next?
- The woman screams and bangs her fists on the locked door. What could happen next?
- The chef slips poison into his boss' soup. What could happen next?

Apply It To Your Story

- Write down each of the plot twists in your story.
- Examine each one to make sure that it is not something the reader will suspect.
- Set a timer and spend 10 minutes brainstorming all of the possible plot twists.
- Write a new plot twist if your brainstorm reveals a better option.

6. Play up the Expectations

Using one of the prompts from number 5, Write a scene that happens before the unexpected plot twist occurs. Refer to your brainstorm list and select one of the first 'expected' ideas. Write a scene leading the reader to believe that the expected thing is going to happen.

For example, your reader may assume that a ship is going to wreck when a sudden storm appears, but the plot twist could be that a pirate ship is going to attack while they focus on the storm.

7. Sprinkle with false suspicion

Rewrite the scene you wrote earlier to redirect the reader with false suspicion. Add details to the scene that lead the reader to believe that what they expect is going to happen. For example, as the storm approaches, the crew prepares to face it. The reader learns that the ship has had mechanical issues in the past.

8. Apply It To Your Work In Progress

It is time for a plot check-up. Examine your plot and your plot twists to make sure you are using the best plot twists possible.

Application Tips & Questions:

- Are your plot points unexpected and surprising?
- If you find a weak plot twist, set a timer for 10 minutes and brainstorm as many alternatives as you can.
- Identify what you want the reader to think is going happen.
- Are there ways you can reinforce the reader's expectation?
- Write or rewrite the plot twist scene.

CHAPTER 5

PROMPTS FOR WRITING DIALOGUE

DIALOGUE SHOULD DRIVE your story forward. These prompts will help you practice your dialogue skills and apply it to your book. Dialogue can play many roles. In this section, you will focus on three different ways that it can move your story forward. Then you will use what you learned to create content for your book or story.

1. Dialogue For Creating Suspense

Select one of the lines below to start your scene. Each line has an element of suspense built into it. Your job is to increase the uncertainty by continuing the dialogue. Set a timer. Write for 5–10 minutes. Every sentence should move the story forward while keeping the reader intrigued.

Select One:

- "The Queen is missing."
- "You can't do that."
- "This is a job nobody wants but ..."
- "This file is corrupt."

- "It's not my blood."

2. Write Dialogue That Creates Conflict

Select one of the dialogue lines below. Write a scene challenging the character's goal. For this exercise, the goal of the character is to get out of a situation. Set the timer for 5–10 minutes.

Select One:

- "You activated the security alarm!"
- "You have my keys."
- "There is no exit."
- "I am going to need you to stay until you finish that."
- "If you leave now, don't come back."

3. Write Dialogue That Reveals

Select one of the scenes below. Set a timer for 5–10 minutes. Write a dialogue scene that reveals what the character wants. You can also build in suspense by letting the dialogue reveal the want.

Select One:

- A truck driver is having engine trouble. A well-meaning motorist stops. The truck driver wants the motorist to leave before he discovers his secret.
- A teen girl is shopping for a dress with her mom. She refuses to try on any of the dresses. She wants her mom to stop making suggestions and ask her what she wants.
- A misunderstood monster comes face-to-face with a terrified child. The beast wants a hug.
- A husband and wife are arguing over what to eat for dinner. The wife wants a take-out pizza, and the husband wants homemade meatloaf.
- Two children are arguing over who made the mess. The

mom wants them to stop arguing and clean up the mess together.
- A customer wants their money back, but the manager refuses.

4. Apply to Your Work in Progress

Select a scene in your story where you can use dialogue to move your plot forward. Decide if you want to create suspense, conflict, or reveal your character's want. It is possible to build all three into the same scene. Set the timer. Write for 5–10 minutes.

When you finish, check the dialogue scene. You can also use these questions to test other scenes:

- Does this dialogue move my story forward? If not, remove it or rewrite it.
- Does this conversation create suspense? If not, is this a place where suspense can improve your story?
- Does this dialogue scene reveal what the character wants?
- Are you presenting new information to the reader?
- Did you include sensory details?
- What do you want the reader to feel while reading this dialogue?

Creative Dialogue Prompts

Use the following prompts as inspiration for new scenes in your current story, or practice what you have learned about writing dialogue or a new story ideas.

- "Nobody forced you to come."
- "Desperate times call for desperate measures."

- "You are the worst vampire I have ever met."
- "The airport is no place for werewolves."
- "Melted crayons are not an excuse for being late."
- "This vacation has become a nightmare."
- "That kid just stuck a cupcake up his nose."
- "You woke me up for this?"
- "I have been living in a tent for five years."
- "The prisoner is missing."
- "I thought she was with you."
- "My parents are monsters."
- "Dig up the grave or lose your life."
- "That is no ordinary valentine."
- "I think I just ate a fly."
- "Schedule the banshee for noon."
- "This is glitter from hell."
- "That beast is actually your grandmother."
- "Respect? I don't have respect for people who eat other humans."
- "What is code magenta?"
- "Don't drink that. It is fuel for my tiny rocket."
- "That cave is really my mom's secret lair."
- "You are a special sort of idiot if you believe that."
- "There is someone hiding in your laundry room."
- "It's not like you are the only one who lost an eye in that fight."
- "She wants you to drive her to the mental hospital."

CHAPTER 6

PROMPTS FOR WHEN YOU ARE STUCK

ARE you stuck in a writing rut? Is your mind spinning with ideas, but you can't move forward with your writing? Are you experiencing writer's block?

Have no fear; the following sections of writing prompts are here to save the day. Some of these will challenge you to examine why you are stuck. Some will allow you to step away from focusing on the stuck part of your story to get your creative flow back on track.

This chapter has two sections. The first contains idea-inducing prompts that you can use to get back into the creative swing of writing.

The second has prompts and exercises that you can apply to your specific book to work through why you are stuck.

SECTION ONE:

Prompts for When You are Stuck and Flexible

1. Fear

It is time to invoke fear in your character. They are having the worst nightmare they have ever experienced. They are unable to wake up.

2. Mommy's Dearest

Pick a character from your story. Write about how they feel about their mother. What negative impacts has she had on them? Positive impacts? Do they see her as a role model or as someone they do not want to be like? Write about how this impacts them and affects what they do.

3. Dialogue Prompts

Select one of the following first lines and write a dialogue scene:

- "You, my dear, are a walking nightmare."
- "That was the worst night of my life."
- "I never thought I would see you in a place like this."
- "Don't even say I told you so."

4. Pathways

Your character is at a crossroad. There are four paths they can take. One path is overgrown with thorn bushes, but they see a town at the end. One path is rocky and steep, and they can't see what is on the other side. The third path is paved but long and winding. The fourth path appears to go back to the place they came from. What path does your character take and why?

5. Rainbows

Your character is mesmerized by a strange creature. They follow it to the end of the rainbow, but what they find is no pot of gold.

6. Silver Linings

Choose an image, object, or situation that is ugly, unappealing, or negative. Write about how your character discovers the good in it. Alternatively, write about how they miss the silver lining.

7. Worst Day Ever

Your character is having the worst day possible. What tragedy starts their day? What happens next, and how does the day get progressively worse?

8. Found objects

Do a web search for strange found objects. Scroll through the results until something catches your interest. Write about it. What is it? Who found it? Where did it come from? What will the finder do with it? How could this object change the world?

9. Never

Make a list of things that your character swears they would never do. Now, force them into a situation where they must do one of those things.

10. Bathroom

Your character is in the bathroom but not for the reason one might think. What is he or she doing in there? What happens if someone barges in and catches them?

11. Pet Cemetery

Your character finds a forgotten pet cemetery. It triggers the memory of a childhood pet that died. What type of animal was it? What happened to it? Write about your character recalling the memory.

12. Backstory Experience

Pick an emotion that your character has trouble expressing. What person, event, or experience from your character's childhood caused the issue?

13. Blank Pages

Your character has been keeping a secret diary, but when they pick it up to write their daily entry, they discover that all the pages are blank. What is their reaction?

14. Blind Date

Your character goes out to meet a friend only to find out they are being set up for a blind date. Write about how they deal with the situation. Will they stay and endure, leave angry, sneak away, or cause a scene?

15. Picture Perfect

Your character is feeling sentimental. They pull out a treasured photograph. Then they notice an alarming detail that they never saw before. What do they see? What questions does this ignite in them? What are they going to do about it? Write a scene showing the progression of emotion from sentimental to another emotion.

16. Dream Catcher

Your character has a reoccurring dream. Write about the dream, how it affects their life, and what caused it. Will it play a part in the story? What if they buy a dream catcher, and instead of catching their bad dreams, it makes them happen?

17. Envelope

An important envelope is missing. Your character is frantic. Write a dramatic scene that reveals the reason behind the drama.

18. Stolen Journal

Your character arrives home from a trip to the coffee shop. When they reach in their backpack, they discover someone's journal. They peek inside to find out who it belongs to and find out the journal contains top secret information.

Congratulations! If you tried at least one prompt and wrote something, you have beat writer's block. If you are still stuck on a specific part of your work in progress, move on to section two.

SECTION TWO:

Prompts and exercises to help you figure out why you are stuck on a particular part of your book or story.

1. Go Back

Pinpoint the part of your story that has you stuck. Now pretend that the last thing that happened did not happen. Brainstorm a list of things that could happen instead of that event.

2. Use the *What If* Method

If you are not sure what to write next, use the *what if* method to generate new ideas. You can use a pen and paper, a mind map app, or type out all of your possibilities.

3. Examine

Examine why you are having trouble writing by answering the following questions:

- What excites me most about this story?
- What do I enjoy most about the characters?
- Why did I decide to write this story?
- What do I not like about my story right now?

- Who am I writing this story for?
- Am I letting perfectionism hold me back from writing?

4. Motives

Is it possible that your story or character has gotten off track? Go back to your character's main goal. Is it still the same? If it has changed, was that your intention? Has your theme or idea for the book changed?

5. Elevator Pitch

If you are stuck, it could be because you don't know exactly where your story is going. This is a good time to go back to basics and work on your Elevator Pitch. An elevator pitch is your novel in 60 seconds or one written page.

6. Outline

If you are stuck, you can refer to your outline. If you don't have one, this is the time to create one. If your story has changed from your original outline, you need to change your outline to fit your story or change your story to fit your outline. Having a detailed outline will allow you to avoid getting stuck because you already know exactly what happens in your story and what you need to write next. Outlines are a guide that can be as flexible or inflexible as you need them to be.

7. Skill Check

Are you stuck because you lack a certain writing skill or knowledge? There are two ways to deal with this issue. The first is to make a note of the issue and skip ahead to a new scene; you will go back and tackle the issue later. The second is to pause your writing and learn what you need to know.

8. Self-care

Are you stuck because you are not taking care of yourself? Have you overworked yourself? If you feel a case of burnout coming on, it is time to take care of yourself. Take a break and allow yourself to rest and recover.

9. Perfection

Are you stuck because you are trying to write the perfect line, the perfect scene, or the perfect book? Reality check: No one is perfect. Writing is a process. Don't expect perfection from your writing and certainly not from your first draft.

10. Perfection Antidote

Go to the part of your writing you are stuck on. Set a timer for 15 minutes. Write the scene as fast as you can and for FUN! Don't worry if it doesn't fit your story. Don't edit, second-guess yourself or stop writing. Once you have written the scene, move on to the next. You can go back and make changes or even rewrite it completely at a later date.

CHAPTER 7

PROMPTS FOR REDISCOVERING YOUR PASSION

DID you start your story with an all-consuming passion for writing it? Did you love your idea, your characters, and all the possibilities? Of course, you did. You are a writer. Writers love new ideas and stories.

Then something changed. At some point, your plot became complicated, tedious and stupid. Your characters don't come across the way you envisioned. Doubt plagues you. You are over the story and clueless about why you thought it was a good idea.

Don't hit the delete key. Don't give up on your book or give in to the temptation to toss your computer in the garbage. Most writers experience this at some point.

It is normal to feel you have lost your excitement for your book. You are knee-deep in the muddy mess of your book. You might be stumbling over plot holes and chasing plot bunnies, but this is no time to give up.

Take time to do some of the following exercises and prompts. They will open your creative flow and reignite your passion for your story. Not all these prompts will find a place in your current story. That is story. This chapter is about exploring the reasons behind your lagging passion.

This section is for you, the writer, to explore your passions and how they relate to your writing.

1. Journal Time

These questions are all about you. They will allow you to examine how you affect the story. Answer the following questions:

- Why did I start writing this story?
- What made me choose this character for this story?
- Who am I writing for?
- How did I get the initial idea for this story?
- How has my initial story idea changed from day one to now?
- How has my idea of my main character changed from day one to now?
- Is there something about this story or character that is frustrating me? What and why?
- What do I want this story to do for the readers?
- What is it about me that enables me to tell this story in a way that no one else can?
- How many hours have I spent working on this?
- Am I willing to sacrifice that time by giving up on my story right now?
- What is the worst thing that will happen if I don't give up on this story?
- What is the best thing that can happen if I don't give up on this story?

2. Vision Board

Consider creating a vision board for your dreams, goals, or for your book. This can be a powerful tool to keep you motivated and reignite your passion when it starts to waver. There are many ways to do this. You can create a virtual vision board with Pinterest. Another option is the traditional vision board. You will need a poster board, photos, magazines, and art supplies.

The goal is to create a visual representation of your vision for your project. Keeping this in front of you allows you to stay on task by reminding you of your goals. The act of creating and focusing on your vision will help you rediscover your passion.

3. Love Lists

Make a list of 10 books, characters, TV shows, and movies you love. Then write out the top 5 things that you love about each one. Do you see a pattern? How can you add these elements to your current work in progress?

4. Hate Lists

Make a list of 5 books, movies, characters, or television shows you hate. Write out the top 5 things you hate about each one. Then scan your work in progress to see if anything from your hate list is present. Cut them if they are contributing to your loss of interest.

5. Memory Lane Lists

It is time to take a trip down memory lane and rediscover the things you loved in your younger days. As we grow, we leave our childhood passions behind us. Exploring the passions of your childhood allows you rediscover yourself. Create a list of things you loved as a child. Here are a few ideas to get you started:

- Favorite Books
- Favorite Authors
- Favorite Games
- Favorite things to pretend

- Favorite magical creatures or powers
- Favorite foods
- The stuff you spent hours doing
- The places you loved to play
- The items you played with
- The things your sibling played with
- The things your parents warned you about
- Your childhood nightmares
- Your childhood fantasies
- Your childhood fears

6. Master List Of Themes

Create a list of themes. You can get started with a internet search or by thinking of themes from books or movies you love. Pick your top 5 favorites. Write about why they appeal to you. Think of the story ideas you have had in the past. Do they fit these themes? Could you take your existing story idea and give it a new spin by changing the theme?

7. Pet Peeves Master List

It is time to explore your pet peeves. Focus on the people, actions, and situations that irritate you. Start by listing as many you can. Then pick a few and expand on them. Write about why they bother you and how you react to them.

8. Personality Clash

Think of three people that you don't click with. Use a mind map to explore all the traits, ticks, and reasons that you are not compatible. The next step is to check your manuscript and characters to discover if any of these traits are interfering with your passion for the story.

9. Vision Check

Remember that Pinterest board you made for your book? This is the perfect time to revisit it. Reviewing what you pinned will reignite your passion for the story and characters. Search for more visual images to add to your board.

10. Vision Statement

Create your author vision statement. What is important to you about writing? Why do you write? What is the purpose behind your story? What do you want the reader to get from your story? Having a clear vision statement will help you stay focused on your writing.

11. Reader Checkup

Who are you writing for? Write a detailed description of who your ideal reader is. Where do they live? What do they look like? What are their hobbies? This is a fun exercise that can also be a valuable tool when marketing your book.

12. Joy Box

Create a scrapbook, journal, or file to store your writing-related accomplishments. Awards, mentions, compliments, book reviews or any tidbit that reminds you of why you write is perfect for your Joy Box.

13. If

If money was no object, and if nothing was standing in your way, what would you do with your day? Where would you live or travel to? Who would be in your life? Exploring the options with no limits is a great way to get in touch with your passions.

14. Personality

Remember the personality test you did for your characters? Getting in touch with your personality type and traits can be a valuable way to rediscover your passions.

15. Values

What are your values? What are the things that are most important to you? List your top ten values. Do any of them play a part in your current book?

16. Book Love

What books and authors have impacted you the most? Make a list that includes the details of why the book impacted you. Start with your favorite books and authors from childhood and continue to the present. What ways have those books shaped you and inspired you to be the writer you are today?

17. Reasons You Write

There are many valid reasons to write, and they are different for everyone. Create a master list of your personal reasons to write. Then write a list of reasons that you want to write the story you are working on now. Include the impact that you want your book to have on the reader.

18. Permission To Suck

Give yourself permission to write badly. Recognize the truth that all books were once someone's badly written first draft. Your first draft is for your eyes only. You are telling the story to yourself. There is plenty of time for revision, editing, and perfecting in the remainder of the writing and publishing process.

19. Partner Up

If you are stuck on a particular part of your story, don't hesitate to reach out to other writers for help. Your critique partners can provide ideas and suggestions because they are looking at your manuscript from a different point of view.

20. Journal

Grab your journal and ask yourself why. Journal and explore your inner thoughts with these creative prompt ideas:

- Why have you lost your passion?
- What is passion?
- What have other people said you are passionate about?
- What makes you excited to wake up in the morning?
- What keeps you up with excitement at night?
- What is the opposite of your passion?
- Are you letting other people discourage you from your passion?
- What is the one thing you can not live with out?
- What passions have you had in the past that are no longer your passion?
- What caused that passion to dry up?
- Have you outgrown a passion that you are still hanging on to?
- Are you resisting your true passion to impress others?
- Are you resisting your true passion because you don't feel you have the needed skills or knowledge?
- How have your passions evolved as you have grown as a person and a writer?
- Do you have passion for a lot of different things? If so, try to focus one passion for a short block of time without letting the other passions prevent you from making progress.
- How does passion or lack of passion impact who you are a person and a writer?

CHAPTER 8
WRITERS TOOL KIT

EVERY WRITER NEEDS A TOOL KIT. A collection of apps, websites, videos, blogs, software, hardware, and things that make the writing process easier to navigate. This is a collection of resources that you can use while writing your fiction book content and with this book

APPLICATIONS

Mind mapping & Brainstorming Apps:

- Free & Paid: www.simplemind.eu
- Free: The timer on your phone.
- Free: Flat Tomato Timer

PERSONALITY TYPES & TESTS

- **Free:** www.16personalities.com
- **Free:** www.howtofascinate.com

AFTERWORD

I hope you have found the prompts in this book as helpful as I and many other writers have. I encourage you to reuse this book of creative prompt ideas whenever you need writing inspiration to create book content or just for fun or skill building.

You Matter. Words Matter. Your Words Matter,

April L. Taylor

http://www.authorapril.com

P.S. As you know, reviews mean the world to authors. If you have found this book helpful, please leave a review on amazon.com and goodreads.com. Your review can be as short or long as you like. You time and effort to leave a review is appreciated and it truly matters.

BONUS PROMPTS

BONUS PROMPTS

I love creating writing prompts. In the process of writing this book, I created some great prompts that did not make it into this book. As a bonus, I am giving you access to over 75 of those prompts when you sign up for my free newsletter. To access your bonus type the link below into your browser.

http://eepurl.com/djWCm9

You have my promise that I will never sell your email or spam you. I strive to provide valuable newsletter content to my subscribers. In addition the valuable content; you will be among the first to have access to all my new books, projects, and life updates.

My mission is always to think of you and treat you as a friend, as a member of my tribe, not just as a subscriber or customer. Because, You Matter. Words Matter. And Your Words Matter.

ACKNOWLEDGMENTS

First of all, this book is dedicated to Leila, for always encouraging and supporting my creativity from the moment I was born and to my love, Vincent for always believing in me.

This book wouldn't have been possible without my amazing critique partners, Ashley, Amber, Allie, & Janine, as well as all of my beta readers and editors.

ABOUT THE AUTHOR

April is a young adult and nonfiction author who loves all things book-related. She wrote her first full length novel at the age of 11 and hasn't stopped writing since.

She a YouTuber who makes writing- and book-related videos. She has a passion for encouraging, coaching, and equipping writers to follow and achieve their writing dreams.

When she is not writing, you can find her plotting her next travel adventure with her fiancé and kids, making a mess with her art supplies, and playing fetch with her cat. Yes, you read that correctly. Her cat loves to play fetch.

She loves making real connections with fellow writers, book lovers, and creatives in real life, on social media, and in fantasy realms.

Sign up for her free newsletter to stay up to date on her writing, books, life and other fun stuff.

www.authorapril.com

Made in the USA
Lexington, KY
09 August 2019